Hello or G'day

English to Australian Slang Dictionary

Enjoy over **1001 +** Aussie slang words

A to Z

Easy to find words and phrase's to impress your friends in Australia and Overseas.

After studying this dictionary and working on a couple other things.

Maybe you can pass as an Aussie in the Big Smoke.

Enjoy

Hooroo

Mr Bennett Books

ENGLISH
TO
AUSTRALIAN
SLANG
DICTIONARY

1001 +
WORDS

A – Z

ENGLISH	AUSTRALIAN
A	A
A lot	Heaps
Abandoned	Alone like a country dunny
Aboriginal (racist term)	Abo
Absolute	London to a brick
Absolutely	Reckon
Abuse	Gobful (give a gobful)
Accountant	Bean counter
Accounting (illegally)	Cook the books
ACDC	Accadacca
Act with attitude	Bung it on
Afternoon	Avro
Agree	Reckon
Agreement (working out)	Nut out
Alcohol	Alkie
Alcohol	Alko
Alice Springs (iconic town)	The Alice
Alone (by yourself)	All alone like a country dunny
Aluminium foil	Alfoil
Amazement	Blimey
Ambulance	Ambo
American	Seppo
Ammunition	Ammo
Angry	Cranky
Angry (exploding with)	Ballistic
Angry getting	Hot under the collar
Angry sounding	Cross as a frog in a sock
Annoyed	Pissed off
Another (one)	Anothery
Answering back	Backchat
Anus	Clacker
Anus	Freckle
Apartment	Flat
Appointment (set up)	Tee-up

Approval	Appro
Army	
(AUS and NZ Army corp.)	A.N.Z.A.C.
Army (reservist)	Cut like a commando
Army reservist	Weekend warrior
Arrive	Rock up
Arse (butt)	Date
Art (enthusiast)	Arty farty
Artist	Arty
Assistant	Offsider
Astounded	Gobsmacked
Attempt	Burl
Attempt (aggressively)	Balls'n all
Australia	Down under
Australia	Aussieland
Australia	The lucky country
Australia	Oz
Australia	Straya
Australia	Bazzaland
Australia (far north)	Top end
Australia capital (territory)	ACT
Australia (interior)	Outback
Australian	Aussie
Australian (genuinely)	Australian as a kangaroo
Australian (truly)	Australian as a meat pie
Australian Broadcasting Corporation	Auntie
Australian man	Bruce
Australian outback	Gaffa
Australian outback (centre)	Never Never
Australian rules football	Footy
Australian rules football	Aerial Ping-Pong
Australian rules football goal posts	Big sticks
Australian slang and pronunciation	Strine
Australian coin game	Two up
Author	Mr. Bennett Books
Avocado	Alligator pear
Avocados	Avos

Bachelors ball	B&S
Baked Beans	Arizona strawberries
Bad luck	Bad trot
Bad mistake	Come a gutser
Bad quality	Bodgy
Bald (no hair)	Bald as a bandicoot
Bald (no hair)	Bald as a badger
Band (pub events)	Muso
Barbecue	Barbie
Barramundi (fish)	Barra
Bartender (woman)	Beer wench
Basic	Bog standard
Bastard	Basket
Bathroom	Shit house
BBQ	Barbie
Beard	Ziff
Beer	Coldie
Beer	Grog
Beer	Piss
Beer	Cold one
Beer	Frothy
Beer	Amber fluid
Beer (285ml glass in NSW)	Middy
Beer **(285ml glass in QLD and VIC)**	Pot
Beer (375ml bottle)	Stubby
Beer (750ml bottle)	Tallie
Beer (750ml in SA)	Long neck
Beer (can cooler sleeve)	Stubby holder
Beer (can)	Tinny
Beer (drank quickly)	Throw-down
Beer (drinking pastime)	Bend the elbow)
Beer (flat of 24)	Slab
Beer (flat of 24)	Block
Beer (large glass)	Pint

Beer (Medium in SA)	Schooner
Beer (open can)	Break open a tinnie
Beer (QLD cheap beer)	XXXX
Beer (small glass in SA)	Butcher
Beer (take away)	Roadie
Beer (time for a)	Beer o'clock
Beer belly	Awning over the toy shop
Beer glass (w/handle)	Handle
Beer Holder	Stubby holder
Beer XXXX	Barbed wire
Behave (aggressive)	Aggro
Behave (foolish)	Act a goat
Belly flop	Belly wacker
Best	Bee's knees
Bet (you)	Betcha
Betting (extravagantly)	Bet like the Watsons
Big City	Big smoke
Big win (sports)	Cream
Bill	Docket
Bird (budgerigar	Budgie
Biscuit	Bikkie
Biscuit (long life cookie)	A.N.Z.A.C Biscuit
Bitch	Bish
Blow fly	Dunny budgie
Blow fly	Blowie
Blow nose (without napkin)	Bushman hankie
Bluebottle jellyfish	Bluey
Blunder	Balls up
Boast	Big-note oneself
Boat (small aluminium)	Tinny
Body board	Boogie board
Bolt (leave quick)	Harold Holt (to do the Harold)
Book maker	Bookie
Bored	Bored shitless
Boring (excessively)	Bore the pants off
Borrow	Bot
Borrow (money)	Bite
Bottle (rhyming slang)	Aristole

Brag	Skite
Brag	Big-note oneself
Brake (hard in automobile)	Hit the anchors
Brake in (w/force)	Barge in
Bread (simple flour and water)	Damper
Bread spread (mmmm)	Vegemite
Breakfast	Brekkie
Breathalyser test	Blow in the bag
Bribe	Backhander
Bricklayer	Brickie
Bright	Cluey
Bring your own drinks	BYO
Brisbane (capital of QLD)	Brizzie
Brisbane (capital of QLD)	Brisvegas
Brisbane cricket ground (Wooloongabba)	Gabba
Brisbane exhibition	Ekka
Broken	Buggered
Buddy	Mate
Bulls eye	Bang on
Bullshit somebody	Raw Prawn (To come the raw prawn)
Bully	Bounce
Bumper (Large grill on automobile)	Roo bar
Bumper (Large grill on truck)	Bull bar
Bundaberg Queensland	Bundy (Where Bundaberg rum is made)
Business	Bizzo
Busy	Cat bury shit (As busy as a cat burying shit)
Busy	Flat out like a drinking lizard
Butterfly	Flutterby
Buttocks	Arse
Buttocks (large)	All behind like a Barney's bull

C	C
Cabernet sauvignon	Cab Sav

Café (cheap)	Chew and spew
Cake	
(Cake in choc and coconut)	Lamingtons
Camouflage (military)	Auscam
Camping bed (canvas roll-out)	Swag
Campfire	Bush telly
Cancel	Bail
Cancer	Big C
Candy	Lollies
Car (American)	Yank tank
Car (Australian make)	Holden
Car (burn out)	Smokie
Car (hood)	Bonnet
Car (old)	Bomb
Car (stuck)	Bogged
Car (truck)	Boot
Car accident (minor)	Bingle
Car registration	Rego
Carburettor	Carbie
Carpenter	Chippie
Carpenter (unqualified)	Bush Chippie
Cat (mixed breed)	Fruit salad
Cattle (round up)	Muster
Cattle (unbranded)	Clean skin
Cattle grazing sites	Long paddock
Caught (doing something wrong)	Sprung
Certainly true	Bloody oath
Chance	Fair go
Chance (very small odds)	Bee's dick
Chat	Chew the fat
Chatter box	Ear bashing
Cheat	Rip off
Cheating	Rort
Cheer	Barrack
Cheerful	Bright spark
Cheque (bad)	Boomerang
Chewing gum	Chewie
Chicken	Chook

Child	Ankle biter
Child (rhyming slang)	Billy lid
Child (small)	Ankle-biter
Child (small)	Carpet grub
Chocolate biscuit	Choccy biccy
Chocolate covered sponge cake	Lamingtons
Chocolate	Chokkie
Christmas	Chrissie
Cigarette	Ciggy
Cigarette	Coffin nail
Cigarette (hand rolled)	Rollie
Chocolate biscuit	Choccy Biccy
Clergyman	Amen snoter
Clothes	Clobber
Clumsy	Cack handed
Cockatoo (bird)	Cockie
Cockroach	Cockie
Coffee (American)	Long black
Coffee (cappuccino)	Flat white
Coffee (iced)	Bogan juice
Coffee break	Smoko
Come on!	Car'n
Complain	Whinge
Complain	Beef
Complain (w/no reason)	Having a whinge
Condom	Franger
Cook (Military)	Bait layer
Cook (rhyming slang)	Babbling brook
Conscientious person	Conch
Cooler	Esky
Corner somebody	Bail up
Corner store	Milk bar
Corrupt	Bent
Cotton candy	Fairy floss
Counterfeit	Brummy
Country people	
(People living in the bush)	Bushie
Cow patties	Field berets

Cow patties	Meadow cakes
Coward	Wuss
Cowboy/girl (cattle rustler)	Duffer (cattle duffer)
Crab (mud crab)	Muddy
Crayfish (inland fresh water)	Yabby
Crazy	Barmy
Crazy	Bats
Crazy	Bonkers
Creeping (on opposite sex)	Perve
Cricket (English supporters)	Barmy Army
Cricket stadium (Perth WA)	WACA (whacker)
Criticize	Knock
Criticize (somebody)	Knocker
Criticize	Rubbish
Criticize (somebody successful)	Tall poppy syndrome
Criticize (to deter)	White ant
Crocodile	Croc
Crocodile (salt water)	Saltie
Crocodile (fresh water)	Freshie
Crowbar	Black snake
Cunning	Dunny rat (Cunning as a dunny rat)
Crayfish (freshwater)	Yabby
C___nt (Used between close friends)	"C" word
Cup of tea	Cuppa

D

D

Dairy farmer	Cow cockie
Damaged	Bung
Dance festival (aboriginal)	Corroboree
Day dreaming	Away with the birdies
Deal	Mates rates
Deceive (lie)	Baffle the bullshit
Defeat (by large margin)	Cream
Defeated	Stonkered

Definitely	Too right
Defrauding	Rort
Delighted	Rapt
Delighted	Pipper (you little ripper)
Deodorant	
(Using instead of shower)	Pommy shower
Depart	Choof off
Depart	Bail out
Devastated	Devo
Disappointment	Blue duck
Diarrhea	Bad case of the trots
Dickhead	Whacker
Die	Cark it
Die	Crock
Difficult (request)	Big ask
Dinner	Tea
Direct route	As the crow flies
Disbelief	Fair suck of the sav
Disbelief	Break it down
Dispute Decision	Argue the toss
Documentary	Doco
Dodgy	Iffy
Dog	Woofer
Dog (Australian sheepdog)	Kelpie
Dog (cattle dog)	Bluey
Dog (cattle dog)	Blue heeler
Dog (mix bred)	Mongrel
Dog (mix bred)	Bitzer
Dog (Native Australian dog	Dingo
Dog (Sheep dog)	Kelpie
Don't like it	Bowl of rice (not my bowl of rice)
Dress (warmly)	Rug up
Diarrhea	Bali belly
Drifter	Bagman
Drink (alcoholic)	Turps
Drink (alone)	Drink with the flies
Drink	
(Bundaberg rum and coke)	Black rat
Drink (chug a beer)	Skull/skol

Drink (excessively)	Bend the elbow
Drinker (heavy)	Booze artist
Drinking (all night party)	Bender
Drinking (binge)	Hit the turps
Drinks (buy the next round)	Shout
Drunk	Face (off one's face)
Drunk	Full
Drunk	Goog (as full as a goog)
Drunk	Gutful of piss
Drunk	Wobbly (he's got the wobbly boots on)
Drunk	Legless
Drunk	Blotto
Drunk	Affluence of inkahol
Drunk (cheap)	Cadbury
Drunk (light weight)	Screamer
Dry	Dead dingo donder (dry as a dead dingo's donger)
Dry	Nun's nasty (dry as a nun's nasty)
Dubious	Shonky
Dud	Also ran
Dumb	Thick as two planks
Dust (outback)	Bull dust

E

E

Earn money	Quid (make a quid)
Easy	Piece of piss
Egg	Cackleberry
Eggs	Bum nuts
Eggplant	Aubergine
Englishman	Bath dodger
Englishman	Pom, pommy or pommie
Englishman	Choom
Englishman (bad)	Pommy bastard
Enthusiastic (yes)	Ken Oath
Environmentalist	Greenie
Erection	Crack the fat
Erection	Stiffy

Erection (state of)	Angle of the dangle
Error	Boo-boo
Event (disappointing)	Bummer
Excellent	Corker
Excellent	Mickey mouse
Excellent	Bonza
Excellent	Ace
Excellent (great)	Spiffy (pretty spiffy)
Excellent (to make it)	Ace it up
Excitable behaviour	Wobbly
Exclamation	Strewth
Exclamation	Cripes
Expensive	Exy

F

F

Fair and square	Cush
Fake	Bodgie up
Fake	Clayton's
Fall over	Arse over tit
Fanatic (religious)	Bible basher
Fantastic	Rip snorter
Fantastic	Beauty
Far off (not going to happen)	Cooee (not within a cooee)
Farm (big)	Station
Farmer	Cockie
Farmer (Hands on boss)	Boss cocky
Fart	Cut lunch
Farted (who did it?)	Who opened their lunch
Feeling (maternal)	Clucky
Fight	Biffo
Fight	Barney
Fight	Blue
Fight (two woman)	Scrag flight
Fight (violent)	Beat the living daylights out of
Finish (what you are doing)	Call it a day
Finished (completely)	All over red rover

Fired	Pink slip (get the pink slip)
Fired	Axe
Fired	Arse out
Fish bait	Berley
Fisherman	Fisho
Flannelette shirt	Flannie or flanno
Flashlight	Torch
Flatter	Crawler
Flirt (romantically)	Crack onto
Flu	Wog
Fly screen	Fly wire
Food bag	Tucker-bag
Fool	Fruit loop
Fool around	Arse around
Foolish	Bent as a scrub tick
Fountain (drinking)	Bubbler
Freeloader	Bludge
French kiss	Pash
Friend	Cobber or mate
Friend	Mate
Friend (best)	Bestest
Friendly (person or animal)	Sook
Frightened	Booby
Frying pan	Banjo
F__k off	Rack off
Full	Choc a bloc
Full house	Chock-a-block
Funny person	Dag
Furious	Berko

G   G

G-strings	Anal floss
G-strings	Bum floss
Gambling	
(Game played on Anzac day)	Two up
Garbage man	Garbo

Garbage truck	Tipper
Garden trimmer	Whipper snipper
Gas	Petrol
Gas station	Servo
Getting (causal)	How ya going (Howzit goin)
Genuine (real deal)	Dinky-di
Get lost	Rack off
Girlfriend	Cliner
Give (something)	Flick
Go away	Bugger off
Go away	Bite your bum
Go cart	Billy cart
God	Big fellow upstairs
Gold prospector	Yellow fever
Golf (swing and miss)	Airy
Good idea	Good oil
Good work	Good on ya
Goodbye	Hooroo
Goof	Dag
Gossip	Chinwag
Government vehicle	Black taxi
Great	Ripper
Great	Beaut or Bonzer
Greatest	Bee's knees
Groupie (female0	Band moll
Guest (uninvited)	Blow-in
Gummy Shark	Flake (used at fish and chip shops)
Gun (rifle)	Bang stick
Gynaecologist	Gyno

H

H

Haircut (poor)	Basin cut
Hammer	American screwdriver
Hangover (drink)	Black aspro
Hat (test cricket hat)	Baggy green
Hard work	Hard yakka

	(work wear clothing company)
Hat (large wide brimmed)	Akubra
Head-butt	Balmain kiss
Helicopter (army or navy)	Angry palm tree
Hello	G'Day
Helmet (bicycle)	Skid lid
Helmet (motorbike)	Brain bucket
Hen	Cook
High (on drugs)	Cooked c__t
High prices	Charge like a wounded bull
Hippie	Feral
Hips (large)	Broad in the beam
Hit	Clobber
Hoarder	Bowerbird
Hobo	Swagman
Hobo (homeless person)	Dero
Homosexual	Backdoor Bandit
Hooligan	Hoon
Horse	Alligator
Horse (rhyming slang)	Apple sauce
Horse (wild)	Brumby
Hospitality Industry	Hospo
Hot dog	Saveloy
Hot water bottle	Hottie

I	I

I don't know	Buggered if I know
Idiot	Whacker
Idiot	Beecham's pill
Ill	Crook
Ill (very)	Cot case
Illegal	Lurk
Information	Drum (I'll give you the drum)
Information (misleading)	Bu'ls wool
Information (useful)	Good oil
Informed	Clued-up

Insane	Around the twist
Insane	Barney as a bandicoot
Insect (repellent)	Aerogard
Insects (biting)	Bities
Insult (friendly)	Mug
Insult (mild)	Ratbag
Interfere	Bib in
Intoxicated	Pissed
It will be OK	Right (she be right)
It'll be all right	Apples, she'll be
Its true	Bloody oath

J	J

Job (high pay)	Cushy
Jockey (Can't stay on horse)	Autumn leaf
Journalist	Journo
Judge	Beak

K	K

Kangaroo	Roo
Kangaroo (baby)	Joey
Kangaroo (family)	Mob
Kangaroo (large male)	Boomer
Kangaroo (red and fast)	Blue flyer
Kerosene	Kero
Kettle (electric)	Jug
Kick	Boot
Kids	Billies
Kilometre	Click
Kindergarten	Kindie
Kiss	Pash
Koala Bear	Billy Blue gum
Koala Bear	Drop Bear

Kookaburra (Australian bird)	Breakfast bird
Kookaburra (Australian bird)	Bushman's alarm clock

L

L

Lake cut off by watercourse	Billabong
Lazy	Slack
Lazy person	Bludger
Leave	Shoot through
Lesbian	Carpet muncher
License plate	Number plate
Lie	Porky
Lie (big)	Boomer
Lifeguard (young surf lifesaver)	Nipper
Linen (house)	Manchester
Lipstick	Lippy
Liquor	Grog
Liquor store	Bottle-o
Listen (attentively)	All ears
Loads	Big mobs
Lobsters	Lobbies
Look	Squizz
Look (take a)(rhyming slang)	Captain Cook (discovered Sydney)
Looking (fabulous)	Ants' pants
Looking lustfully (opposite sex)	Perve
Lookout (illegal)	Cockatoo
Loser	Dipstick
Loss your temper	Blow a fuse
Lost something	Gone walkabout
Lotto ticket (instant)	Scratchy
Lucky	Tin-arsed
Lucky	Cop it sweet
Lunch	Tea
Lunch (at desk when working)	Al desko

M

M

Machine (powerful)	Beast
Mailman	Postie
Male	Bloke
Man	Bloke
Man (big belly)	Beer gut
Man (helpful)	Bottling (his blood's worth bottling)
Man (sissy)	Big girl's blouse
Man (strong)	Brick shit house (built like a brick shit house)
Map of Tasmania	Mappa Tassie
Maple syrup	Cocky's joy
Marble (large)	Bonker
Marijuana	Mull
Marriage (problems)	Caustic crackers and strawberry sand
Masturbation	Bat
McDonald's	Maccas
Mean	Cat's piss (as mean as cat's piss)
Measurement (early unit of)	Axe handle
Meat pie	Dog's eye
Melbourne (Australia)	Athens to the south
Mentally unstable	Bananas
Methylated sprits	Metho
Military Service (compulsory)	Nasho
Milkman	Milko
Mistake	Blunder
Mistake	Clanger
Mistake	Blue
Mobster	Stand over man
Moment (any moment now)	Any tic of the clock
Money	Moolah
Money	Axle grease
Money (fifty note)	Banana
Money (five cents)	Zack
Money (lots)	Big bickies
Money (ten note)	Blue swimmer
Money (wasted)	Blow your dough

Mongrel	Bitser
Mouth	Cake hole
Move away from the tropics	Troppo gone
Moving (at great speed)	Bat out of hell
Mosquito	Mozzie
Motorcycle gang member	Bikie
Murrumbidgee river (Australia)	Bidgee
Muscle	Beef
Mythical outback creature	Bunyip

N

N

Nagging	Ear bashing
Naked	Nuddy (in the nuddy)
Naked	Birthday suit
National anthem	Advance Australia Fair
National service	Nasho
Nauseating	Chunderous
Nerd	Dag
Nervous	Crack the shits
Neutral (gear in automobile)	Angel gear
New South Wales resident	Cornstalk
New South Wales residents	Cockroach
New Zealander	Sheepshagger
Next (in line)	Bags I go next
No chance	Buckley's chance
No problem	No drama
No problem	No worries
Northern Australia	Top end
Nose	Beak
Nose	Bugle
Not happy	Spewin
Not functioning	Cactus
Nothing	Bugger all

O

O

Obsequious	Brown nose
Obvious	Dog's balls (stands out like)
OK	Apples
Opinion	Bob's worth
Original	Ridgy-didge
Outback	
(Anywhere there isn't a town)	Bush
Outback creature (mythical)	Bunyip
Outhouse (bathroom)	Dunny
Outlaw	Bushranger
Over protective	Clucky
Overcoming hardship	Little Aussie battler
Overly dramatic	Carry on like a pork chop
Overseas	O.S.

P

P

Packed	Chocker's
Pants	Strides
Pants (trousers)	Daks
Parents	Oldies
Pardon	Ay
Parents (elderly)	Crumblies
Parking ticket	Blister
Partner (male or female)	Better half
Parrot (small)	Budgie
Party	Rage
Party (most social occasions)	Piss up
Party (bring own food)	Plate (bring a plate)
Party (large)	Going off
Party (late into the night)	Rage on
Party (wild)	Bash
Patriotic	True blue
Pavlova (New Zealand dessert)	Pav
Pay back	Alley up

Penis	Donger
Penis	Doodle
Penis	Old fella
People (group)	Mob
People (successful)	Tall poppies
People	
(QLD/NSW Boarder towns)	Mexican
Perplexed	Stonkered
Person (brainless)	Air head
Person	
(Chinese born in Australia)	ABC
Person (irreverent)	Buggerlugs
Person (despicable)	Mongrel
Person (disgusting)	Animal
Person (disruptive)	Yobbo
Person (excellent)	Boddy dazzler
Person (fool)	Drongo
Person (good-looking)	Spunk
Person (idiotic)	Cough drop
Person (know it all)	Aleck
Person (Idiot)	Dill
Person (lazy)	Bludger
Person (loser)	Dropkick
Person (loud)	Yobbo
Person (Mediterranean)	Wog
Person (mentally inadequate)	Kangaroos loose in the top paddock
Person (mentally inadequate)	Not the full quid
Person (meticulous)	Anally retentive
Person (nosy)	Sticky beak
Person (old/crabby)	Battle-axe
Person (ordinary)	Copper tail
Person (overweight)	Built like the side of a house
Person (Prude)	Wowser
Person (really unattractive)	Bags rough as
Person (rowdy)	Yobbo
Person (silly)	Galah (Australian bird)
Person (skinny)	All prick and ribs
Person (stupid)	Alf
Person (stupid)	Drongo

Person (tall/lanky)	Bean pole
Person (unattractive)	Head like a dropped pie
Person (uncouth)	Yobbo
Person (uncultured)	Bevan
Person (unsophisticated)	Ocker
Person (W/ high opinion of themselves)	Figjam
Person or animal (Coward)	Wuss
Person or thing (incompetent)	Useful as an ashtray on a motorbike
Person or thing (unhelpful)	Useful as tits on a bull
Perth WA (cool breeze from Freemantle)	Freemantle doctor
Perth WA (Freemantle)	Freo
Person (Acting overly dramatic)	Carry on like a pork chop
Phone	Al Capone
Phone call	Bell
Phone somebody	Give somebody a bell
Pickup truck	Ute
Play house	Cubby House
Playing games	Mucking around
Pleased	Rapt
Police	Blues
Police (patty wagon)	Booze Bus
Police (prison bus)	Divvy van
Police (ticket)	Bluey
Policemen	Coppers
Politician	Polly
Pond (inside a dry riverbed)	Billabong
Poor (very)	Brass razoo
Popsicle	Icy pole
Porch (w/bed)	Sleep out
Porn movie	Blue movie
Position	Pozzy
Potato	Murphy
Potato	Spud
Potato chips	Crisps
Prankster	Larrikin
Present	Prezzy
Prison	Bin

Prison	Bluestone college
Promoter (outside nightclub)	Spruiker
Propane	Gas
Prospector	Fossick
Prostitute	Chromo
Pub	Boozer
Pub (rough)	Blood house

Q

Q

Quality (bad)	Shit house
Queenslander	Banana-bender
Queenslander	Cane toad

R

R

Rabbit	Underground mutton
RAAF (Australian Air force)	Adgie
Rally race	Bush bash
Real	Fair Dinkum
Reasonable	Fair suck of the sauce
Reassurance	No worries
Receipt	Docket
Redhead	Blue
Redhead	Bushfire blonde
Redhead	Bluey
Redneck	Bogan
Refugee	Reffo
Refuse	Knock back
Registration (automobile)	Rego
Relative (cousin, aunt or uncle)	Rellie or relo
Relax (w/TV)	Veg out
Repeat (yourself)	Beg yours
Reprimand (severely)	Blow the shit out of somebody
Rest (short)	Breather

Ridiculous	All wet
Ripper	Bonzer
River (full to edge)	Banker
Road (tarmac)	Bitumen
Rubbish	Bull dust
Rugby union team (New Zealand)	All Blacks
Rugby union team (Australia)	Wallabies
Rumour	Furphy

S

S

Salt water crocodile	Saltie
Salvation Army	Salvos
Sandals	Thongs
Sandwich	Sanger
Sandwiches	Cut lunch
Sharks	After Darks
Satisfied	Grinning like a shot fox
Sausage	Banger
Sausage	Mystery bag
Sausage	Snag
Scratch and win ticket	Scratchy
Scrounger	Botfly
Search	Fossick
Seat (back of bus)	Backseat bogan
Seconds (w/food)	Back up to
Self controlled (obsessively)	Anal
Sell (quick flip)	Flick it on
Semi Truck (W/two or more trailers)	Road train
Setback	Come a cropper
Seven Eleven (store)	Bevan Heaven
Sex	Root
Sex	Buffin' the muffin
Sex (have)	Naughty (have a naughty)
Sex (somebody looking for)	Rat root

Sexually (experienced)	Been around
Shaky	Wonky
Sheep	Jumbuck
Sheepskin boots	Ugg boots
Sheets (linen)	Manchester
Shelter (camp)	Bandicoot gunyah
Shit (noisy or smelly)	After-grog bog
Shocker (rhyming slang)	Barry Crocker
Show how things work	Show you the ropes
Shower (w/deodorant only)	Pommy shower
Shut up	Bite your bum
Sick	Crook
Sick Day (when you are fine)	Chuck a sickie
Sick Day (when you are fine)	Sickie
Sideboard (cupboard)	Duchess
Silly	All froth and no beer
Semi tuck (w/many trailers)	Road train
Sister	Blood and blister
Skipping school	Waggin' school
Sleeping bag	Matilda
Sleeping bag (tough outdoor)	Swag
Slot machines	Pokies
Slot machines	Fruit machines
Slow in the head	Bourke street (Doesn't know ___ from Bourke St)
Small child	Ankle biter
Small town	Woop woop
Sneakers	Runners
Snitch	Dob (Dob somebody in)
Snot (nasal mucus)	Bush oyster
Social assistance (Using when not needed)	Dole bludger
Socks	Almond rocks
Solider	Digger
Somebody (low IQ)	Quid (not the full quid)
Somebody (socially awkward)	Piker
Somebody (That never does well)	No-hoper
Somebody	

(Tries to impress others)	
Somebody	
(W/high opinion of oneself)	Tickets (to have on oneself)
Somebody	
(You don't agree with)	Pig's arse
Something awesome	She's a bloody ripper
Something excellent	Bottler
Something of very little substance	Airy fairy
South Australian resident	Pie eater
South Australian resident	Crow eater
South Australian residents	Crow eater
Spaghetti (Bolognese)	Spag bol
Speak (Idly)	Bat the breeze
Speed (fast)	Billyo
Speedo (men's swimsuit)	Budgie smugglers
Speedometer	Speedo
Speedos	Budgie smugglers
Spinsters ball	B&S
Spoiled	Cactus
St. Vincent de Paul's	
(Thrift shop)	Vinnie's
Stag party	Buck's night
Stairs	Apples and Pears
Start eating	Bog in
Station hand (female farmer)	Jillaroo
Station hand (male farmer)	Jackaroo
Statement (gutsy)	Big call
Steal	Flog
Stop functioning	Clark it
Stubborn	Bloody-minded
Student (agriculture)	Aggie
Substitute	Clayton's
Suburbs (outside)	Back blocks
Suit (rhyming slang)	Bag of fruit
Suitcase	Port
Sunbathe	Sunbake
Sunglasses	Sunnies
Support (team)	Barrack
Surfer	Surfies

Surfer (beginner)	Shark biscuit
Surprise	Crickey
Surprise (exclamation)	Holy dooley
Surprise (exclamation)	Strewth
Surprised	Gobsmacked
Surprised (expression)	Stuffed (I'll be stuffed)
Suspicious	Dodgy
Sweater	Jumper
Sweets	Lollies
Swimming Costume	Bathers
Swimsuit	Cozzie
Sydney harbour bridge	Coat hanger

T   T

Tackle (hard)	Bone crusher
Taking advantage of somebody	Lend of (to have a lead of)
Talk (with no action)	All piss and wind
Take away shop (food)	Milk bar
Take out (food)	Snatch and grab
Talker	Yabber
Tantrum	Chuck a wobbly
Task (easy)	Piece of piss
Tasmania (Australia)	Apple isle
Tasmanian resident	Apple eater
Tasmanian resident (Derogatory term)	Taswegian
Teacher	Chalkie
Teacup (tin for camping)	Billy
Teapot	Billy
Tease	Chiack
Teeth (rhyming slang)	Barrier reef
Teeth	Choppers
Teeth	Clackers
Term of endearment	Bastard
Termites	White ants
Terrific	Bargain

Terrific	Grouse
Testicle	Ball
Testicles	Apricots
Thank you	Ta
Thingummyjig	Doovalacky
Thirsty (to be very)	Dry as a bark hut
Thrift store	Op shop
Throat	Angora Goat
Throwing stick (Aboriginal hunting tool)	Boomerang
Ticked	Sucked in
Tip off	Drum (I'll give you the drum)
Tired	Stuffed (I feel stuffed)
Tired	Zonked
Toast spread (Australian)	Vegemite
Tobacco	Baccy
Tobacco	Durry
Toilet	Dunny
Toilet	Bog house
Toilet paper	Bog roll
Tomato sauce (ketchup)	Dead horse
Tool box (tradesman)	Bag of tricks
Top student	Dux (he duxed his final)
Topless sunbathers	White pointers
Tracksuit	Trackies
Tracksuit pants	Trackie daks
Tramp	Swagman
Tricked	Sucked in
Trouble	In the shit
Trouble (serious)	Blue murder
Truce	Barley
Truck	Ute
Truck driver	Truckie
Truth (True)	Fair Dinkum
True (undeniably true)	Deadset
Try	Bash
Try it	Give it a burl
Try something	Av-a-go-yer-mug

Truancy (skip school)	Wag
Turd in sea or pool	Brown-eyed mullet or Bondi cigar
Turpentine	Turps
TV	Idiot box

U

U

U-turn	Yewy
U-turn	Chuck a u-ey
Ugly	Ugh
Umbrella	Brolly
Unattractive	Head like a dropped pie
Understand	Cotton on to
Underwear	Grundies
Unexpected	Boil-over
Unfortunate	Fuck me dead
University	Uni
Unstable	Wonky
Unsteady	Wonky
Upset (getting angry)	Spit the dummy
Upside down	Base over apex
Urinal puck	Trough lolly
Urinate	Piss
Urinate (when swimming)	Aqua bog

V

V

V 8 Truck	
(W/redneck upgrades)	Feral
Van (multi purpose)	Kombi
Van (one tonne)	Comby
Vegetables	Veggies
Vegetarian	Veggo
Vegetarian	Wombat
Very	Bloody

Very	Bloody
Very Angry	Cut Snake (mad as a cut snake)
Very angry	Ropeable
Very angry	Spewin'
Very dry	Pommy towel (As dry as a pommy towel)
Very good friend	Clobber
Very good	Ace
Very happy	Grinning like a shot fox
Very Happy	Rapt
Very long way away	Back of Bourke Or Beyond the black stump
Very Obvious	Shang on a rock (Stands out like a shag on a rock)
Very pleased	Stoked
Very poor	Brass Razoo (He hasn't got a brass razoo)
Very strong	As fit as a mallee bull
Very upset at something	Dummy (split the dummy)
Victorian resident	Cabbage patcher
Visit somebody	Lob (lob in)
Volkswagen	Vee dub
Vomit	Chunder
Vomit	Liquid laugh
Vomit	Technicolor yawn
Vomit (outside)	Bark on the lawn
Vulgar	Lair
Vulgar manner	Lair it up

W	W

Wadjamacallit	Thingo
Wait (a moment)	Arf-a-mo
Walk in the outback	Walkabout
Warm dress	Rug up
Water	Adam's ale
Waving (At flies around you)	Salute (Aussie salute)

Wedding Day	Big day
Well done	Good onya
Western Australian resident	Sandgroper
What do you think	What di ya reckon
Who cares	Big woop
Wholeheartedly	Boots and all
Wife	Ball and chain
Wife	Cook
Wine (cheap)	Plonk
Wine (no label)	Cleanskin's
Wine box	Chateau de cardboard
Wine box	Briefcase
Wine cask (racist term)	Aboriginal suitcase
Wishing somebody bad luck	May your chooks turn into emus and kick your dunny door down
Woman	Sheila
Woman	Babe
Woman (aggressive)	Ball tearer
Woman (any age)	Boiler
Woman (old)	Biddy
Woman (pregnant)	Bun in the oven
Woman (unattractive)	Bag
Woman public space	Mappa Tassie
Women (promiscuous)	Bangs like a dunny door in the wind
Women's underwear	Knickers
Work	Yakka
Work (ineffectually)	Bugger about
Worker (unskilled)	Blue-tongue
Workers compensation pay	Compo
Working hard (For little money)	Battler
Worn out	Clagged out
Wrench	Spanner

X

X

XXXX Gold

XXXX Heavy

Y

Yawn	Dingo's breakfast
You	Ya
You (plural)	Youse
Young surfer	Grommet

Z

Zero	Zilch

Ta and Hooroo

Mr Bennett Books

www.ingramcontent.com/pod-product-compliance
Lightning Source LLC
Chambersburg PA
CBHW052042280526
45791CB00010B/3056